The HEART of JESUS

A DEVOTIONAL JOURNAL

The HEART of JESUS

from *The Jeremiah Study Bible*

DR. DAVID JEREMIAH

WORTHY

Copyright © 2013 by David Jeremiah, Inc.

ISBN 978-1-61795-090-2
ISBN 978-1-61795-320-0 (retail exclusive)

Published by Worthy Publishing, a division of Worthy Media, Inc.
134 Franklin Road, Suite 200, Brentwood, Tennessee 37027.

Scripture quotations are from the New King James Version of the Bible. Copyright © 1979, 1980, 1982 by Thomas Nelson, Inc., publishers. Used by permission.

Cover Design by Jeffrey Jansen, Aesthetic Soup
Page Layout by Bart Dawson

Printed in the United States of America

1 2 3 4 5—HaHa—17 16 15 14 13

INTRODUCTION

The Good Shepherd. The Prince of Peace. The Living Word. Although Jesus is known by many names, He has one heart, and it's revealed throughout the pages of the Bible. This devotional gives you sixty ways over sixty days to get to know Him better.

Drawn from passages throughout the Gospels, you'll interact with verses in which Jesus reveals something about Himself—His purposes, His priorities, His parables, His prayers. Each devotional will whet your appetite for further study, beginning with the three questions we should always be asking when facing God's Word:

- What does it say?
- What does it mean?
- What does it mean for me?

As you search for Jesus' heart over the next sixty days, your heart will be changed. That's the power of His Word. That's my prayer for you.

—*Dr. David Jeremiah*

The HEART of JESUS

1

JOHN 8:56–59

"Your father Abraham rejoiced to see My day, and he saw it and was glad." Then the Jews said to Him, "You are not yet fifty years old, and have You seen Abraham?" Jesus said to them, "Most assuredly, I say to you, before Abraham was, I AM." Then they took up stones to throw at Him; but Jesus hid Himself and went out of the temple, going through the midst of them, and so passed by.

I AM

When Jesus was born in Bethlehem, He did not begin; He had always been. When Jesus made this statement to the Pharisees, they were confounded. How could Jesus, in His thirties, be older than Abraham? But they missed the whole point. Jesus was saying that before He was born in Bethlehem, He eternally existed. He is the eternal Son of God. What a magnificent occasion when Deity invaded humanity, and eternity invaded time.

The seven "I Am" sayings of Jesus in the book of John:

- "I AM the bread of life" (6:35).
- "I AM the light of the world" (8:12; 9:5).
- "I AM the door" (10:7, 9).
- "I AM the good shepherd" (10:11, 14).
- "I AM the resurrection and the life" (11:25).
- "I AM the way, the truth, and the life" (14:6).
- "I AM the true vine" (15:1, 5).

QUESTIONS

What It Says: How does Jesus' claim compare to God's words in Exodus 3:14?

_____

_____

_____

_____

What It Means: Why was the reaction of the religious leaders to stone Jesus?

_____

_____

_____

_____

What It Means for You: What do these I AM statements teach about the relationship He wants to have with you?

_____

_____

_____

_____

_____

2

LUKE 2:8–14

Now there were in the same country shepherds living out in the fields, keeping watch over their flock by night. And behold, an angel of the Lord stood before them, and the glory of the Lord shone around them, and they were greatly afraid. Then the angel said to them, "Do not be afraid, for behold, I bring you good tidings of great joy which will be to all people. For there is born to you this day in the city of David a Savior, who is Christ the Lord. And this will be the sign to you: You will find a Babe wrapped in swaddling cloths, lying in a manger." And suddenly there was with the angel a multitude of the heavenly host praising God and saying: "Glory to God in the highest, And on earth peace, goodwill toward men!"

ANGELS SAY

Historically, a shepherd was one of the lowest jobs one could do, so it was relegated to the outcasts and those who couldn't hold any other jobs. Yet these people were the audience for heaven's most amazing announcement. The good tidings of great joy were to *all* people, even those with little or no social standing.

There are three components to the angels' message:

- A song of praise—"Glory to God!"
- A song of peace—"On earth peace."
- A song of purpose—"Goodwill toward men!"

The message of the gospel is that humanity is no longer at enmity with the Almighty; God's Son has torn down those barriers. "Having been justified . . . we have peace with God" (Rom. 5:1), and there is "no condemnation for those who are in Christ Jesus" (Rom. 8:1).

QUESTIONS

What It Says: Who were the first to learn that Messiah had been born?

_____

_____

_____

What It Means: They must have doubted their eyes and ears. What information did the angel give them so they could verify the announcement?

_____

_____

_____

What It Means for You: Why is peace with God so precious?

_____

_____

_____

3

MATTHEW 2:1–2, 9–10

Now after Jesus was born in Bethlehem of Judea in the days of Herod the king, behold, wise men from the East came to Jerusalem, saying, "Where is He who has been born King of the Jews? For we have seen His star in the East and have come to worship Him." . . . and behold, the star which they had seen in the East went before them, till it came and stood over where the young Child was. When they saw the star, they rejoiced with exceedingly great joy.

HIS STAR

The star shining in the East wasn't just any star. According to Matthew 2:2, it was *His* star, supernaturally placed in the heavens for the purpose of guiding the wise men. This is nothing new. Throughout biblical history, God guides His people. He led Abram away from everything he knew, promising to show him the way (Gen. 12:1). He directed Moses from a burning bush (Ex. 3:2), then led His children through the wilderness with a cloud by day and a pillar of fire by night (Ex. 13:21).

While God is sovereign and infinite, we see that He is also a personal and loving Father who promises to guide and direct our lives. Psalm 119:105: "Your word is a lamp to my feet and a light to my path." When we live according to God's Word, He is able to direct our steps.

QUESTIONS

What It Says: How did the wise men know that a king had been born?

_____

_____

_____

_____

_____

What It Means: Why was Jerusalem their initial destination?

_____

_____

_____

_____

_____

What It Means for You: Looking back at your life, have there been times when unusual circumstances guided your path?

_____

_____

_____

_____

_____

4

MATTHEW 2:11

And when they had come into the house, they saw the young Child with Mary His mother, and fell down and worshiped Him. And when they had opened their treasures, they presented gifts to Him: gold, frankincense, and myrrh.

SYMBOLIC GIFTS

While we do not know how many wise men there were, we do know that the three gifts they gave to Jesus were especially appropriate because of their symbolism. One was a gift of gold, fit for a king. Gold—pure, valuable, and nearly indestructible—is indeed a royal metal, and in the ancient world, it was even rarer than it is today. Frankincense was a gift for a priest, since it was mixed with oil and used to anoint priests. The final gift was myrrh, a gift for the Savior. The term comes from the Hebrew term *mar*, which means "bitter." Myrrh was used to prepare dead bodies for burial; the corpse was wrapped in layers of cloth and spices were placed between the layers to cover the odor of decay. This final gift foreshadowed the suffering Jesus would endure on the cross in fulfillment of His role as Savior.

QUESTIONS

What It Says: Can you imagine a foreign delegation showing up at your house?

_____

_____

_____

_____

What It Means: These gifts were rare and valuable, but the road they foretold wasn't an easy one. What lay ahead for this innocent Child?

_____

_____

_____

_____

What It Means for You: What gifts have you been given that are fitting for the role God has for you?

_____

_____

_____

_____

_____

5

LUKE 2:46–51

Now so it was that after three days they found Him in the temple, sitting in the midst of the teachers, both listening to them and asking them questions. And all who heard Him were astonished at His understanding and answers. So when they saw Him, they were amazed; and His mother said to Him, "Son, why have You done this to us? Look, Your father and I have sought You anxiously." And He said to them, "Why did you seek Me? Did you not know that I must be about My Father's business?" But they did not understand the statement which He spoke to them. Then He went down with them and came to Nazareth, and was subject to them, but His mother kept all these things in her heart.

FROM A BOY TO A MAN

Luke tells a story from the childhood of Jesus in which we glimpse His future destiny and greatness. It includes His very first recorded words. In His childhood, Jesus subjected Himself to the limitations of being human. He came to earth as an infant, and He experienced normal development; He would have been indistinguishable from all of the other children of His day.

The Incarnation would be meaningless had Jesus not grown up in ordinary ways. Luke 2:16 refers to Him as "the Babe." In Luke 2:27 and 40, He is called "the Child." In Luke 2:43, He is called "the Boy." And in Luke 2:48, He is called "Son." These are terms of graduated growth—from a babe to a son of the law, the *bar mitzvah*. Nevertheless, Jesus was perfcct at every stage of His life, transitioning from stage to stage without imperfection.

QUESTIONS

What It Says: What are Jesus' first recorded words?

_____

_____

_____

What It Means: How did Jesus' perspective differ from that of His parents?

_____

_____

_____

What It Means for You: Would you find it convicting to raise a perfect child?

_____

_____

_____

_____

_____

JOHN 20:30–31

Truly Jesus did many other signs in the presence of His disciples, which are not written in this book; but these are written that you may believe that Jesus is the Christ, the Son of God, and that believing you may have life in His name.

THAT YOU MAY BELIEVE

The Gospels don't necessarily give an exact chronology. Though each Gospel has a logical flow, the writers' primary goal wasn't to describe events in the order they occurred. Instead, each wrote with a unique purpose. The Gospel of John was written to prove that Jesus is God. Mark wrote his Gospel to demonstrate that Jesus Christ was a servant. In his Gospel, Luke dealt with the humanity of Christ; he wrote to reveal Jesus Christ as the Son of Man. Matthew wrote his Gospel to prove, beyond any doubt, that Jesus was the Messiah, the King of Israel.

The writers could only include so much in their accounts. As John says, "And there are also many other things that Jesus did, which if they were written one by one, I suppose that even the world itself could not contain the books that would be written. Amen" (John 21:25).

QUESTIONS

What It Says: What was the purpose behind the writing of this Gospel?

_____

_____

_____

_____

What It Means: How does your perspective on these stories change when you know that there's an underlying purpose to the miracles?

_____

_____

_____

_____

What It Means for You: If belief means life, how do these Gospels change how you live?

_____

_____

_____

_____

_____

JOHN 1:40–46

One of the two who heard John speak, and followed Him, was Andrew, Simon Peter's brother. He first found his own brother Simon, and said to him, "We have found the Messiah" (which is translated, the Christ). And he brought him to Jesus. Now when Jesus looked at him, He said, "You are Simon the son of Jonah. You shall be called Cephas" (which is translated, A Stone). The following day Jesus wanted to go to Galilee, and He found Philip and said to him, "Follow Me." Now Philip was from Bethsaida, the city of Andrew and Peter. Philip found Nathanael and said to him, "We have found Him of whom Moses in the law, and also the prophets, wrote—Jesus of Nazareth, the son of Joseph." And Nathanael said to him, "Can anything good come out of Nazareth?" Philip said to him, "Come and see."

COME AND SEE

People come into a personal relationship with Jesus Christ in a variety of ways. First, we see from the life of John the Baptist that salvation sometimes comes through the preaching of the Word. In the story of Andrew and his brother Simon Peter, we learn that sometimes the concern of a family member is all that's needed for us to meet Christ. As we take the time to tell our loved ones about Jesus and all He has done for us, they may respond to the gospel. From Philip, we see that salvation may come through a pointed encounter with the Savior. While we may not think of God intervening directly in our lives, He may choose to speak to us at any time, as He did with Philip. And then in the story of Nathanael, we see that salvation can come through the powerful testimony of a friend.

QUESTIONS

What It Says: In what ways did the good news spread?

_____

_____

_____

What It Means: Do you trust a friend's recommendation over mass advertising? Why?

_____

_____

_____

What It Means for You: How many ways and places can you think of in which you could spread the word about Jesus?

_____

_____

_____

_____

_____

8

MARK 2:3–5

Then they came to Him, bringing a paralytic who was carried by four men. And when they could not come near Him because of the crowd, they uncovered the roof where He was. So when they had broken through, they let down the bed on which the paralytic was lying. When Jesus saw their faith, He said to the paralytic, "Son, your sins are forgiven you."

BRING THEM TO JESUS

The four friends in this story show Christians how to encourage those who may not know Jesus. We cannot save them, but we can bring them to the Savior.

1. *Through intercession.* We bring our friends to Jesus as we intercede for them and as we plead for their salvation.
2. *Through conversation.* Our openness about our faith and willingness to naturally share who Jesus is in any kind of interaction with our friends invites them to Him.
3. *Through invitation.* We can bring them to Jesus as the four men did in this circumstance, only we'll pick them up in our car and bring them to church. We can make sure we meet them in the lobby and sit with them in the service so they won't feel alone. We can introduce them to others who will make them feel welcome.

QUESTIONS

What It Says: How far were these four men willing to go for their friend?

_____

_____

_____

_____

What It Means: What does Jesus see?

_____

_____

_____

_____

What It Means for You: In what ways can your faith extend to your unsaved friends or family? How can you carry them to Jesus?

_____

_____

_____

_____

_____

_____

9

MARK 1:35–37

Now in the morning, having risen a long while before daylight, He went out and departed to a solitary place; and there He prayed. And Simon and those who were with Him searched for Him. When they found Him, they said to Him, "Everyone is looking for You."

A MATTER OF FAITH

Jesus habitually prayed in a solitary place before His day began so that He could commune with His Father and prepare Himself for the challenges ahead. He *often* withdrew from the whirlwind of a popular ministry to get alone with His Father (Luke 5:16). Despite the never-ending demands of ministry, He never sacrificed this discipline, and it resulted in extraordinary power.

Prayer is a matter of faith: taking God at His word and trusting His promise to work on His people's behalf—even when His work is invisible, when the answers are long in coming, and when He seems to be withholding His blessings. As followers of Christ we need a time to listen for the *Father's* will for our lives (Matt. 26:39, 44). If Jesus needed times of solitude and prayer, how much more do His followers!

QUESTIONS

What It Says: Name a few of the obstacles Jesus had to overcome to find some alone time.

_____

_____

_____

_____

What It Means: What is the purpose of prayer?

_____

_____

_____

_____

What It Means for You: Where is your quiet place?

_____

_____

_____

_____

_____

10

MARK 4:37-41

And a great windstorm arose, and the waves beat into the boat, so that it was already filling. But He was in the stern, asleep on a pillow. And they awoke Him and said to Him, "Teacher, do You not care that we are perishing?" Then He arose and rebuked the wind, and said to the sea, "Peace, be still!" And the wind ceased and there was a great calm. But He said to them, "Why are you so fearful? How is it that you have no faith?" And they feared exceedingly, and said to one another, "Who can this be, that even the wind and the sea obey Him!"

WEATHERING STORMS

The storm on the Sea of Galilee reminds readers that no one is exempt from life's storms just because he or she follows Christ. As was true for the disciples here, tempests can burst upon His people's lives even when they are near Him. Rough weather should never surprise us (1 Pet. 4:12–13). In fact, Scripture says that storms must come our way if we want to live a godly life (2 Tim. 3:12).

When Jesus and the disciples shoved off from the shore that day, He knew the storm was coming, yet He didn't prevent it. Why? First, He knew He would be with them through it. Second, He knew that a life without turmoil has no real meaning, no real joy, and produces no real faith. Christians must remember that Jesus is present. He is in control; nothing surprises Him. He has not forgotten us, or our plight.

QUESTIONS

What It Says: How does Jesus' response to the storm compare to that of His disciples?

_____

_____

_____

_____

What It Means: Why the Lord compare their fear with a lack of faith?

_____

_____

_____

_____

What It Means for You: Do you find it more difficult to trust God in life's big things or in the little things?

_____

_____

_____

_____

_____

_____

11

LUKE 5:27–28

After these things He went out and saw a tax collector named Levi, sitting at the tax office. And He said to him, "Follow Me." So he left all, rose up, and followed Him.

WALK AWAY

Sometime during his life, Matthew had left his Jewish religion behind. The lure of wealth as an agent of Rome overpowered whatever commitment he might have had to the tenets of Judaism, until Jesus issued a startling invitation.

Matthew was sitting in his tax booth, possibly calculating the day's take, when the itinerant preacher everyone was talking about strode purposefully up to his makeshift office, looked him right in the eyes, and said, "Follow Me." And just that quickly, Matthew did! He stood up, stepped out from behind the counter, and walked away . . . *from everything.* As Scripture says, Matthew "left all, rose up, and followed Him."

Scripture gives us no hint of hesitation. When Jesus looked at him and called his name, Matthew instantly turned his back on his old life and became a lifelong disciple of the young rabbi from Nazareth.

QUESTIONS

What It Says: What did Jesus invite Matthew to do?

_____

_____

_____

_____

What It Means: Matthew's life has a dramatic before and after. What came before this choice? How much of his future can he see?

_____

_____

_____

_____

_____

What It Means for You: When do you find it hard to let go of things?

_____

_____

_____

_____

_____

_____

12

LUKE 6:19–23

Then He lifted up His eyes toward His disciples, and said: "Blessed are you poor, For yours is the kingdom of God. Blessed are you who hunger now, For you shall be filled. Blessed are you who weep now, For you shall laugh. Blessed are you when men hate you, And when they exclude you, And revile you, and cast out your name as evil, For the Son of Man's sake. Rejoice in that day and leap for joy! For indeed your reward is great in heaven, For in like manner their fathers did to the prophets."

BLESSED ARE . . .

Jesus' followers wanted dominion and prosperity; Jesus' teachings speak of poverty and sorrow. For many, these words—known as the Beatitudes—were like cold water on the hot enthusiasm people had for the kingdom. They were certain that the kingdom would make them free and rich, and Jesus turned all of their expectations upside down (Matt. 5:1–12).

- *The humble.* Those with destitute hearts sense their spiritual need and seek after God (Ps. 34:18; 51:17).
- *The hurting.* The one who weeps over the pains of life can be confident of God's healing and comfort.
- *The harnessed.* Meekness implies a humble acceptance of one's lowly position before God.
- *The hungry.* These people seek God in whose presence "is fullness of joy" (Ps. 16:11).

- *The helpers.* Mercy manifests in practical, compassionate, and cheerful love toward those suffering.
- *The holy.* These people have guileless motives, holy thoughts, and a clean conscience.
- *The healers.* Peacemakers help others reconcile with God and with one another.
- *The harassed.* Persecution is suffering wrongfully, being punished for being righteous.

QUESTIONS

What It Says: Why would the Beatitudes cool the enthusiasm of many of Jesus' audience?

_____

_____

What It Means: What kind of people does God honor? Where is their heart? Where are their priorities?

_____

_____

What It Means for You: Can you see yourself in this list? Which of these promises is most precious to you personally?

_____

_____

13

MATTHEW 5:13–16

You are the salt of the earth; but if the salt loses its flavor, how shall it be seasoned? It is then good for nothing but to be thrown out and trampled underfoot by men. You are the light of the world. A city that is set on a hill cannot be hidden. Nor do they light a lamp and put it under a basket, but on a lampstand, and it gives light to all who are in the house. Let your light so shine before men, that they may see your good works and glorify your Father in heaven.

SALT AND LIGHT

Salt has a number of characteristics that illustrate the Christian's role in the world. It hinders the spread of corruption; it creates thirst; and it enhances flavor. Christians who live out the virtues described in the Beatitudes achieve all three of these purposes. "Walk in wisdom toward those who are outside, redeeming the time. Let your speech always be with grace, seasoned with salt, that you may know how you ought to answer each one" (Col. 4:5, 6).

Jesus' purpose is to be a "light to the Gentiles [nations]" (Isa. 42:6; Luke 2:32). Here, He confers the same task on His followers. Christians must allow God's light to be on full display in their lives. Their responsibility is twofold: to guard against anything that can separate them from their only source of light, and to let their light so shine that others will see the reality of Christ in them and glorify their heavenly Father.

QUESTIONS

What It Says: What does Jesus equate light with?

_____

_____

_____

_____

What It Means: Why doesn't Jesus expect His followers to blend into the crowd?

_____

_____

_____

_____

What It Means for You: If your behavior reflects on God's reputation, how should you live? What might you think twice about saying or doing?

_____

_____

_____

_____

_____

14

MARK 1:40–42

Now a leper came to Him, imploring Him, kneeling down to Him and saying to Him, "If You are willing, You can make me clean." Then Jesus, moved with compassion, stretched out His hand and touched him, and said to him, "I am willing; be cleansed." As soon as He had spoken, immediately the leprosy left him, and he was cleansed.

JESUS AND THE LEPER

The first miracle Matthew records is Jesus' healing of a man with leprosy (Mark 1:40; Luke 5:12). All such infected individuals were required to stay away from healthy men and women (Lev. 13:45–46); but this man disregarded that instruction and instead directly approached Jesus. He clearly believed Jesus had the power to heal him; he simply did not know if the Lord had a *desire* to do so.

Any Jew who touched a leper was declared ceremonially unclean and unfit to worship with the congregation of Israel. Notice that Jesus touched this leper, making Himself "unclean" and exposing Himself to the disease. But Jesus' touch indicated His authority over all disease, and the leper was immediately made whole. With the touch, Jesus healed the man fully—physically and emotionally.

QUESTIONS

What It Says: What does this miracle tell us about Jesus?

_____

_____

_____

_____

What It Means: What areas of life were lepers banned from? How much did he lose when he was diagnosed with this disease?

_____

_____

_____

_____

What It Means for You: Haven't we also been made clean? What changes does that make for your life?

_____

_____

_____

_____

_____

15

MARK 4:1–3, 9

And again He began to teach by the sea. And a great multitude was gathered to Him, so that He got into a boat and sat in it on the sea; and the whole multitude was on the land facing the sea. Then He taught them many things by parables, and said to them in His teaching: "Listen! Behold, a sower went out to sow. . . ." And He said to them, "He who has ears to hear, let him hear!"

LISTENING AND HEARING

Someone has defined a parable as an earthly story with a heavenly meaning. The word literally means "brought alongside." So a parable takes something that is understood (a simple story or word picture) and uses it to illustrate something that is not understood (a truth). In essence, a teacher using a parable is saying, "You don't understand what I'm saying? Okay, it is like this . . ."

Jesus begins His parable with a challenge to listen and ends it with His frequent exhortation to hear His words. This phrase usually accompanies a saying or parable that is not self-explanatory. Casual listeners could not expect to mine the riches of His teachings. Even the disciples could not discern the meaning of the parable. This is a good example for all Christ followers: continue to seek answers and ask the Lord for understanding when a biblical teaching is unclear.

QUESTIONS

What It Says: What was Jesus' teaching style?

_____

_____

_____

_____

What It Means: How did he make faith something people could grasp?

_____

_____

_____

_____

What It Means for You: When you run up against something that's hard to understand, how do you usually respond?

_____

_____

_____

_____

_____

_____

16

MATTHEW 13:34–35

All these things Jesus spoke to the multitude in parables; and without a parable He did not speak to them, that it might be fulfilled which was spoken by the prophet, saying: "I will open My mouth in parables; I will utter things kept secret from the foundation of the world."

WORD PICTURES

The two wisest men who ever lived—Solomon and Jesus—shared a unique trait: they were both master teachers who employed word pictures to convey truth. In His stories Jesus describes the poor breaking bread, patching garments, and sweeping the floor. There is a king marching to war, a rich man with his barns bursting with increase, a poor widow begging for help from a judge, and two debtors in contrast to each other. His parables describe a Pharisee and a tax collector praying in the temple. There are flocks and herds, birds and flowers.

Jesus takes common things that the Jewish people would have known well and constructs a short story within which He communicates something His listeners do not know. For those with open ears and open hearts, He unveils more than a new understanding; He reveals a whole new kingdom—the kingdom of heaven.

QUESTIONS

What It Says: How often did Jesus speak in parables?

_____

_____

_____

_____

What It Means: What can a story reveal?

_____

_____

_____

_____

What It Means for You: Why is there a wisdom in connecting heavenly things to earthly ones?

_____

_____

_____

_____

_____

_____

MARK 4:10–13

But when He was alone, those around Him with the twelve asked Him about the parable. And He said to them, "To you it has been given to know the mystery of the kingdom of God; but to those who are outside, all things come in parables, so that 'Seeing they may see and not perceive, And hearing they may hear and not understand; Lest they should turn, And their sins be forgiven them.'"

ILLUMINATE AND FRUSTRATE

Sometimes Jesus used parables to hide the truth from the spiritually prideful. God had closed the spiritual eyes and ears of many in Israel because of sin (Isa. 5–6). As a result, most Jewish leaders did not recognize Jesus when His earthly ministry began. For them His words were like a foreign language, the language of the kingdom of God. He often spoke in parables so that the Jewish leaders could not access the truth, which was of no interest to them anyway.

By teaching in parables, Jesus both illuminated the hearts of the spiritually sensitive and frustrated the minds of the spiritually blind. The same parable could be a blessing or a curse, depending on the mind of the person who was listening. And the same is true today. The greatest temptation when we read the stories of Jesus is to read them as entertainment. But they are so much more.

QUESTIONS

What It Says: If you turn around Mark 4:12, how can the truth change its hearer?

_____

_____

_____

_____

What It Means: Have you ever talked to someone who refuses to listen, especially about spiritual things?

_____

_____

_____

_____

What It Means for You: What is your motive in studying the words of Jesus? Have you been changed by what you learned?

_____

_____

_____

_____

_____

18

MATTHEW 9:1–6

So He got into a boat, crossed over, and came to His own city. Then behold, they brought to Him a paralytic lying on a bed. When Jesus saw their faith, He said to the paralytic, "Son, be of good cheer; your sins are forgiven you." And at once some of the scribes said within themselves, "This Man blasphemes!" But Jesus, knowing their thoughts, said, "Why do you think evil in your hearts? For which is easier, to say, 'Your sins are forgiven you,' or to say, 'Arise and walk'? But that you may know that the Son of Man has power on earth to forgive sins."

ARISE

When these men brought Jesus a paralytic lying on a bed, He said, "Arise, take up your bed, and go to your house" (Matt. 9:7). The response was immediate. The paralytic stood up and walked home, and the onlookers were amazed. "When the multitudes saw it, they marveled and glorified God, who had given such power to men" (Matt. 9:8). But they missed the significance of the miracle.

Jesus responded to those gathered in three extraordinary ways:

- He saw the faith in the hearts of the four men (v. 2);
- He saw the sin in the heart of the paralytic and forgave him (v. 2); and
- He saw the unbelief in the hearts of the scribes (v. 4).

Jesus did it not to demonstrate that God had given such power to men, but to demonstrate that God's presence was among them in Him.

QUESTIONS

What It Says: What are the undercurrents running through this scene?

_____

_____

_____

What It Means: Why did Jesus say He was going to heal the man? How is this different from why the people were rejoicing?

_____

_____

_____

What It Means for You: Jesus clearly understood the hearts of all those around him, yet He was misunderstood. How well do you understand what God has said?

_____

_____

_____

_____

MATTHEW 9:35–38

Then Jesus went about all the cities and villages, teaching in their synagogues, preaching the gospel of the kingdom, and healing every sickness and every disease among the people. But when He saw the multitudes, He was moved with compassion for them, because they were weary and scattered, like sheep having no shepherd. Then He said to His disciples, "The harvest truly is plentiful, but the laborers are few. Therefore pray the Lord of the harvest to send out laborers into His harvest."

MOVED WITH COMPASSION

Compassion suggests strong emotion and means "to feel deep sympathy." Jesus saw these people as weary and scattered . . . sheep without a shepherd (Num. 27:17; 1 Kings 22:17; Ezek. 34:5; Zech. 10:2) because the religious leaders, who should have been their shepherds, were trying to lead them away from the one true Shepherd.

"Behold, I say to you, lift up your eyes and look at the fields, for they are already white for harvest! And he who reaps receives wages, and gathers fruit for eternal life, that both he who sows and he who reaps may rejoice together" (John 4:35–36). Because Jesus saw the great need of the multitude, He urged His disciples to pray to the Lord of the Harvest for more laborers. That prayer, which is at the core of the modern missions movement, is still the only hope for the lost sheep of each generation (Eph. 4:11–12).

QUESTIONS

What It Says: What sparked our Shepherd's compassion?

_____

_____

_____

_____

_____

What It Means: What does this tell us about His hopes for all people?

_____

_____

_____

_____

_____

What It Means for You: When can you sow? Where do you harvest?

_____

_____

_____

_____

_____

20

MARK 4:14–20

The sower sows the word. And these are the ones by the wayside where the word is sown. When they hear, Satan comes immediately and takes away the word that was sown in their hearts. These likewise are the ones sown on stony ground who, when they hear the word, immediately receive it with gladness; and they have no root in themselves, and so endure only for a time. Afterward, when tribulation or persecution arises for the word's sake, immediately they stumble. Now these are the ones sown among thorns; they are the ones who hear the word, and the cares of this world, the deceitfulness of riches, and the desires for other things entering in choke the word, and it becomes unfruitful. But these are the ones sown on good ground, those who hear the word, accept it, and bear fruit: some thirtyfold, some sixty, and some a hundred."

THE FRUIT OF TRANSFORMATION

Jesus explains that the Word gets various receptions, although ultimately, the only reception that bears fruit is to hear it and accept it. Some hearers are hardened, so the seed of the Word doesn't even make an impression. Others seem to take in the Word but their commitment to the gospel soon disappears in times of trouble. For some, worldly concerns and distractions overwhelm what they know, so they never put the Word into practice.

Of the four soils, only this good ground produces the fruit of transformation—and it does so despite the seduction of riches and

the difficulties of life. Where God's Word is wanted, He makes sure it is never wasted. Those who apply Jesus' words to their lives are given even more spiritual truth, making their lives richer.

QUESTIONS

What It Says: What obstacles rise up to prevent us from listening to or applying God's Word?

_____

_____

_____

What It Means: As believers, we may hear the Word, but what does it mean to accept it?

_____

_____

_____

What It Means for You: Do you want to bear fruit? How can you tend to the soil of your heart to make sure the Word isn't wasted?

_____

_____

_____

_____

21

MATTHEW 11:28–30

Come to Me, all you who labor and are heavy laden, and I will give you rest. Take My yoke upon you and learn from Me, for I am gentle and lowly in heart, and you will find rest for your souls. For My yoke is easy and My burden is light.

COME TO ME

Come—or more literally, "Come now!"—is one of the most gracious commands in the Bible. Jesus' invitation speaks to all who are oppressed by routine, monotony, overwork, responsibility, and tension. Those who are heavy laden endure something that is laid on them from an outside source, causing what we would today call "burnout." Jesus' form of rest is not absence of work but rejuvenation and refreshment.

In Jesus' day, taking the yoke of another meant coming under that person's leadership and walking in that person's footsteps (Phil. 2:5; 1 Pet. 2:21; 1 John 2:6). When believers take Jesus' yoke, they place themselves under His dominion (John 8:29). Only then do His followers enjoy the day-by-day release from stress that God intended. "For this is the love of God, that we keep His commandments. And His commandments are not burdensome" (1 John 5:3).

QUESTIONS

What It Says: How does Jesus describe Himself? Who does He say needs Him?

_____

_____

_____

_____

What It Means: There's an opportunity to learn from Jesus in this invitation. What can we learn from Him?

_____

_____

_____

_____

What It Means for You: What burdens are you carrying right now?

_____

_____

_____

_____

_____

LUKE 5:36–39

Then He spoke a parable to them: "No one puts a piece from a new garment on an old one; otherwise the new makes a tear, and also the piece that was taken out of the new does not match the old. And no one puts new wine into old wineskins; or else the new wine will burst the wineskins and be spilled, and the wineskins will be ruined. But new wine must be put into new wineskins, and both are preserved. And no one, having drunk old wine, immediately desires new; for he says, 'The old is better.'"

A NEW WAY

The unshrunk piece of cloth represents the promised kingdom; the old garment represents Judaism. Jesus knew that to marry grace to the law would be like sewing patches from new, unshrunk cloth onto an old garment. When the fabric was washed, the patches would shrink, rip away, and ruin the whole garment. Jesus did not come to patch up Judaism but to introduce the gospel of grace, a wholly new thing.

Likewise, Jesus did not come to reform people but to redeem them. To follow Jesus requires a radical break with the old way of life; any attempt to mix the old with the new is bound to fail, bringing a worse situation than previously existed (Heb. 10:11–23). Salvation is not an improvement of the old nature. Salvation is a new nature, which is accompanied by the presence of the Holy Spirit (1 Cor. 3:16; Col. 3:9, 10).

QUESTIONS

What It Says: Why can't you blend the old ways with the new way?

_____

_____

_____

_____

What It Means: Can you think of a modern parable for this same principle?

_____

_____

_____

_____

What It Means for You: Many people create a patchwork faith, mixing pieces and parts of different beliefs to build one that suits them personally. What's the inevitable end of their efforts?

_____

_____

_____

_____

23

LUKE 6:12–16

Now it came to pass in those days that He went out to the mountain to pray, and continued all night in prayer to God. And when it was day, He called His disciples to Himself; and from them He chose twelve whom He also named apostles: Simon, whom He also named Peter, and Andrew his brother; James and John; Philip and Bartholomew; Matthew and Thomas; James the son of Alphaeus, and Simon called the Zealot; Judas the son of James, and Judas Iscariot who also became a traitor.

THE TWELVE

Luke writes that Jesus spent the night in prayer before choosing His twelve apostles. He called people from all walks of life. In this group of select apostles were fishermen, a political revolutionary (zealot), and a despised tax collector (Matthew). One denied the Lord (Peter), one was known as the doubter (Thomas), two had trigger-tempers (James and John, "Sons of Thunder," Mark 3:17), and one lived in infamy as a traitor. Yet this unlikely crew changed the world.

As apostles (literally, "sent ones"), they first had to be with Jesus for an extended period of time; then He would send them to preach, to heal various sicknesses, and to cast out demons as His ambassadors. By virtue of their intimate connection to Him, all of Jesus' followers are able to represent Him to a lost and hurting world (John 15:1–8).

QUESTIONS

What It Says: What criteria did Jesus use when choosing His disciples?

_____

_____

_____

_____

What It Means: Is our mission any different from that of the Twelve?

_____

_____

_____

_____

What It Means for You: Why is it an honor to be recognized, trusted, chosen? Do you have a position like this now?

_____

_____

_____

_____

_____

_____

_____

24

MARK 3:31–35

Then His brothers and His mother came, and standing outside they sent to Him, calling Him. And a multitude was sitting around Him; and they said to Him, "Look, Your mother and Your brothers are outside seeking You." But He answered them, saying, "Who is My mother, or My brothers?" And He looked around in a circle at those who sat about Him, and said, "Here are My mother and My brothers! For whoever does the will of God is My brother and My sister and mother."

BROTHER, SISTER, MOTHER

At this stage of His ministry, not even Jesus' family believes that He is the Messiah, the Chosen One of God. In Mark 3:21, we read, "But when His own people heard about this, they went out to lay hold of Him, for they said, 'He is out of His mind.'" He faced opposition and doubt from His own people and, eventually, from within the Twelve, not just from the religious teachers and His political enemies. Still, Jesus never wavered from His mission.

A closer bond exists between brothers and sisters in the Christian faith than among biological siblings because believers share a spiritual relationship. This is why Jesus later says that believers who must part ways with their family of origin because of their faith gain a much larger and more closely knit family (Mark 10:29–30).

QUESTIONS

What It Says: How did Jesus redefine family for His followers?

_____

_____

_____

_____

What It Means: Jesus never wavered from His mission, but what did that cost Him?

_____

_____

_____

_____

What It Means for You: What promise does Mark 10:29–30 hold for you? Who are your brothers, sisters, mothers, and fathers in the faith?

_____

_____

_____

_____

_____

25

MATTHEW 6:25, 31-34

Therefore I say to you, do not worry about your life, what you will eat or what you will drink; nor about your body, what you will put on. Is not life more than food and the body more than clothing? . . . Therefore do not worry, saying, "What shall we eat?" or "What shall we drink?" or "What shall we wear?" For after all these things the Gentiles seek. For your heavenly Father knows that you need all these things. But seek first the kingdom of God and His righteousness, and all these things shall be added to you. Therefore do not worry about tomorrow, for tomorrow will worry about its own things. Sufficient for the day is its own trouble.

WHY DO YOU WORRY?

In Matthew 6:25–34, Jesus says, "Do not worry" three times, and He gives five reasons why we should not worry:

1. *Worry is inconsistent* (6:25). If we can trust Jesus to provide us with our life, can we not also trust Him with our daily needs?
2. *Worry is irrational* (6:26). If our Lord cares for the birds, will He not also care for us, since we are more valuable than birds?
3. *Worry is ineffective* (6:27). Who among us can add one cubit (the length from the elbow to the tip of the middle finger) to our stature by worrying?
4. *Worry is illogical* (6:28–30). If God can clothe the lilies of the field, can He not also clothe us?

5. *Worry is irreligious* (6:31–32). When we worry, we act just like those who do not know God.

QUESTIONS

What It Says: What does Jesus say life is more than?

_____

_____

_____

What It Means: What kinds of worries are basic to all people?

_____

_____

_____

What It Means for You: List some of the worries that creep in to your thoughts. How do these feelings affect your day? What do they steal from you?

_____

_____

_____

_____

_____

26

MARK 10:17, 19–22

Now as He was going out on the road, one came running, knelt before Him, and asked Him, "Good Teacher, what shall I do that I may inherit eternal life?" . . . You know the commandments: 'Do not commit adultery,' 'Do not murder,' 'Do not steal,' 'Do not bear false witness,' 'Do not defraud,' 'Honor your father and your mother.'" And he answered and said to Him, "Teacher, all these things I have kept from my youth." Then Jesus, looking at him, loved him, and said to him, "One thing you lack: Go your way, sell whatever you have and give to the poor, and you will have treasure in heaven; and come, take up the cross, and follow Me." But he was sad at this word, and went away sorrowful, for he had great possessions.

ONE CAME RUNNING

In the ancient Middle East, it was considered undignified for a man to run; however, this man threw his respectability to the wind, rushed to Jesus, and fell on his knees before Him. This man recognized that he was missing something important—eternal life—but he did not understand that salvation is about what God does for sinners rather than what they do for God.

Because Jesus loved this man, he called him to the truth of uncompromising discipleship: nothing less would do than to leave behind all that mattered to him—both the wealth and the social position that came with it—in exchange for eternal life. The term translated sad means more literally, "to cloud up." The young ruler's problem was not riches themselves but that he trusted in such things, believing that life with God could somehow be bought.

QUESTIONS

What It Says: What commandments was this man able to say he kept?

_____

_____

_____

What It Means: Yet he knew something was missing? What did he want from Jesus?

_____

_____

_____

What It Means for You: Looking back at your life, what makes you "cloud up"? What do our regrets teach us about what we truly value?

_____

_____

_____

_____

_____

27

MARK 10:21–22

Then Jesus, looking at him, loved him, and said to him, "One thing you lack: Go your way, sell whatever you have and give to the poor, and you will have treasure in heaven; and come, take up the cross, and follow Me." But he was sad at this word, and went away sorrowful, for he had great possessions.

THE PULL OF POSSESSIONS

The Bible presents no data to support the idea that being wealthy is wrong. In fact, we find evidence to the contrary: "The blessing of the Lord makes one rich, and He adds no sorrow with it" (Prov. 10:22). Scripture also offers many notable examples of godly, wealthy people—Job, Abraham, Nicodemus, Jesus' friends Mary, Martha, and Lazarus, as well as Joseph of Arimathea, Barnabas, and Philemon.

So God does not disapprove of people with money. But He does speak out against those who rely on riches, as this young man did. In the first-century world, for a wealthy man to give up all his possessions meant a demotion in social class. He would need to start a whole new life in a community that refused to make money the basis of its pecking order. So in effect, this rich young ruler's priorities were the problem, not his possessions.

QUESTIONS

What It Says: What was Jesus' attitude toward this young man?

_____

_____

_____

_____

_____

What It Means: What was the trade-off the rich young ruler faced?

_____

_____

_____

_____

_____

What It Means for You: Are there things you enjoy giving to others? Are there things that are more difficult to share?

_____

_____

_____

_____

_____

28

MATTHEW 9:14–15

Then the disciples of John came to Him, saying, "Why do we and the Pharisees fast often, but Your disciples do not fast?" And Jesus said to them, "Can the friends of the bridegroom mourn as long as the bridegroom is with them? But the days will come when the bridegroom will be taken away from them, and then they will fast."

FASTING

Nothing was wrong with fasting, so long as it supported its true purpose: allowing a person to repent or focus more deeply on God. But the Pharisees fasted ritualistically—not from the heart—never realizing that God cannot be manipulated. According to the law, Jews were required to fast only one day each year: the Day of Atonement. The Pharisees, however, had extended that law to require twice-weekly fasts.

Jesus and His disciples did not follow their fasting laws, and John's disciples wanted to know why. Jesus answered with a wedding analogy. Fasting during a wedding feast is inappropriate. John the Baptist had already announced that Jesus was the Bridegroom, and when the Bridegroom is present, people celebrate. Soon the Bridegroom would be taken away, and then it would be proper to mourn and fast.

QUESTIONS

What It Says: Who is questioning Jesus?

What It Means: Is there a difference between ritual and discipline?

What It Means for You: Have you ever gone through the motions of faith without knowing the joy it's supposed to bring? Why are you able to celebrate with your Bridegroom?

29

LUKE 9:23-26

Then He said to them all, "If anyone desires to come after Me, let him deny himself, and take up his cross daily, and follow Me. For whoever desires to save his life will lose it, but whoever loses his life for My sake will save it. For what profit is it to a man if he gains the whole world, and is himself destroyed or lost? For whoever is ashamed of Me and My words, of him the Son of Man will be ashamed when He comes in His own glory, and in His Father's, and of the holy angels."

A CRUCIFIED LIFE

The person who desires to follow Jesus must set aside their own agenda in order to completely comply with God's agenda. To voluntarily and daily take up one's cross points to the Roman practice of forcing condemned criminals to carry part of the tool of their execution to their place of death. Followers of Christ must not only give up their own agenda but die to it.

Jesus gave two compelling reasons for choosing the "crucified life" over a life dedicated to pursuing one's own agenda. First, pursuing selfish gain is no life at all. Second, even if someone could amass all the wealth and privilege the whole world has to offer, it would be a foolish choice, because the price is one's own soul. When Jesus returns in power and glory, He will openly reward all who identified with Him, regardless of the temporary price they paid.

QUESTIONS

What It Says: What do we have to lose? What do we have to gain?

_____

_____

_____

_____

What It Means: What happens to those who willingly identify themselves with Jesus?

_____

_____

_____

_____

What It Means for You: How do you deal with embarrassment? What do you do when you're ashamed of something?

_____

_____

_____

_____

_____

30

MARK 12:41–44

Now Jesus sat opposite the treasury and saw how the people put money into the treasury. And many who were rich put in much. Then one poor widow came and threw in two mites, which make a quadrans. So He called His disciples to Himself and said to them, "Assuredly, I say to you that this poor widow has put in more than all those who have given to the treasury; for they all put in out of their abundance, but she out of her poverty put in all that she had, her whole livelihood."

TREASURY BOXES

The collection plates in Jesus' day were big boxes fitted on top with large horns that resembled the speaker of an antique gramophone. People would drop their tithes and offerings into this funnel, which would direct the money into a receptacle. Some ostentatious worshipers brought as many coins as they could carry, standing back some distance from the box and throwing their offering into the trumpetlike horn so that the sound of their coins would echo throughout the great stone building for bystanders to hear.

Jesus warned against these showy displays. "Beware of the scribes, who desire to go around in long robes, love greetings in the marketplaces, the best seats in the synagogues, and the best places at feasts, who devour widows' houses, and for a pretense make long prayers. These will receive greater condemnation" (Mark 12:38–40). Having the appearance of faith isn't the same as trusting God.

QUESTIONS

What It Says: Is it not a good thing that many people gave much money?

_____

_____

_____

_____

What It Means: When is it hardest to be generous with what you have?

_____

_____

_____

_____

What It Means for You: What does a "good person" look like in this day and age? Is it any different than what a "successful" person looks like?

_____

_____

_____

_____

31

MATTHEW 14:14–21

And when Jesus went out He saw a great multitude; and He was moved with compassion for them, and healed their sick. When it was evening, His disciples came to Him, saying, "This is a deserted place, and the hour is already late. Send the multitudes away, that they may go into the villages and buy themselves food." But Jesus said to them, "They do not need to go away. You give them something to eat." And they said to Him, "We have here only five loaves and two fish." He said, "Bring them here to Me." Then He commanded the multitudes to sit down on the grass. And He took the five loaves and the two fish, and looking up to heaven, He blessed and broke and gave the loaves to the disciples; and the disciples gave to the multitudes. So they all ate and were filled, and they took up twelve baskets full of the fragments that remained. Now those who had eaten were about five thousand men, besides women and children.

A FEAST

The call to extend godly compassion does not depend on circumstances. Jesus had just lost His beloved cousin, the Jewish leaders were plotting against Him, and He knew what lay ahead in Jerusalem. Yet moved with compassion, He stopped to meet the needs of the crowd, healing their sick.

There was no food for the hungry crowd, yet Jesus told his disciples to give them something to eat. God often gives His children tasks they cannot complete with their own strength. The loaves and fish, which seemed insufficient from a human perspective, were more than enough for Jesus to feed the crowd (John 15:5; Phil. 4:13). The disciples only saw the poverty of their limited resources, but with twelve baskets left over, Jesus may have been signaling that this feast was Israel's—a basket for every tribe.

QUESTIONS

What It Says: Why did Jesus ask His disciples to do the impossible?

_____

_____

_____

What It Means: Do we limit God by focusing on what can't be done?

_____

_____

_____

What It Means for You: Has there been a time in your life when your needs were met right when they were greatest?

_____

_____

_____

_____

32

MATTHEW 14:22–27

Immediately Jesus made His disciples get into the boat and go before Him to the other side, while He sent the multitudes away. And when He had sent the multitudes away, He went up on the mountain by Himself to pray. Now when evening came, He was alone there. But the boat was now in the middle of the sea, tossed by the waves, for the wind was contrary. Now in the fourth watch of the night Jesus went to them, walking on the sea. And when the disciples saw Him walking on the sea, they were troubled, saying, "It is a ghost!" And they cried out for fear. But immediately Jesus spoke to them, saying, "Be of good cheer! It is I; do not be afraid."

EXHAUSTED RESOURCES

Jesus had told the disciples to row across the lake around 5 or 6 p.m. He had gone to the mountain nearby to pray from early evening until 3 a.m. Why did Jesus allow His followers to struggle in isolation for seven or eight hours? If He had rescued them immediately, the disciples might forget His intervention or perhaps assume that, given enough time, they could have saved themselves.

When the disciples saw someone walking across the surface of the water, they were afraid not only because they suspected a ghost. Mark says it was also because their hearts were hard (Mark 6:52). Even though they had just witnessed the miraculous feeding of a multitude, they failed to apply that experience of Jesus' power to this situation. The Lord sometimes waits until His followers have exhausted their resources before He steps in.

QUESTIONS

What It Says: What must this storm have been like if seasoned fishermen feared for their lives?

_____

_____

_____

_____

What It Means: If there are indeed twelve baskets of bread with them in the boat, what have the disciples lost sight of?

_____

_____

_____

_____

What It Means for You: Have you ever forgotten about God's past provision when a new problem arises?

_____

_____

_____

_____

_____

33

MATTHEW 14:28–33

And Peter answered Him and said, "Lord, if it is You, command me to come to You on the water." So He said, "Come." And when Peter had come down out of the boat, he walked on the water to go to Jesus. But when he saw that the wind was boisterous, he was afraid; and beginning to sink he cried out, saying, "Lord, save me!" And immediately Jesus stretched out His hand and caught him, and said to him, "O you of little faith, why did you doubt?" And when they got into the boat, the wind ceased. Then those who were in the boat came and worshiped Him, saying, "Truly You are the Son of God."

TAKE MY HAND

What people focus on becomes magnified, especially in fearful circumstances, and the wind caught Peter's attention. Whenever believers divert their eyes from Jesus in the midst of a storm, their circumstances assume prominence, and they, like Peter, lose heart and begin to sink. The difference between fear and faith is focus.

Peter was not acting foolishly, and this was not a daring stunt; it was obedience. When Jesus beckoned him to come, Peter willingly went. What's more, he did not fail that day; the failures were the other disciples who stayed in the boat where they thought they were safe. They failed to experience the joy of walking on water and the hand of Jesus reaching out to them in their time of need. It is tempting to look down on sinking Peter for his small faith, but at least he was willing to step out of the boat!

QUESTIONS

What It Says: What destroyed Peter's focus?

_____

_____

_____

_____

What It Means: Where were the disciples placing their trust?

_____

_____

_____

_____

_____

What It Means for You: Is your own faith as unsteady as a storm-tossed boat? What's the solution?

_____

_____

_____

_____

_____

_____

34

LUKE 12:6–7

Are not five sparrows sold for two copper coins? And not one of them is forgotten before God. But the very hairs of your head are all numbered. Do not fear therefore; you are of more value than many sparrows.

SPARROWS

In the midst of discussing the dangers they would face, Jesus comforted His disciples with the knowledge that they never escape God's notice. He argued from the lesser to the greater. Sparrows were the cheapest meat sold in the market. "Are not two sparrows sold for a copper coin? And not one of them falls to the ground apart from your Father's will" (Matt. 10:29). Jesus also told them, "You will be hated by all for My name's sake. But not a hair of your head shall be lost" (Luke 21:17–18).

If every hair is numbered, and every sparrow is accounted for, then certainly He will not forget His dear children in their trials, for they are worth far more.

QUESTIONS

What It Says: Nothing, no one, is beneath God's notice. Why would this comfort Jesus' disciples?

_____

_____

_____

_____

What It Means: Since what you learn now may be needed later, what sorts of things do you want to study and journal about for future use?

_____

_____

_____

_____

What It Means for You: Have you ever not wanted to bother God with little things?

_____

_____

_____

_____

_____

35

MATTHEW 16:24–27

Then Jesus said to His disciples, "If anyone desires to come after Me, let him deny himself, and take up his cross, and follow Me. For whoever desires to save his life will lose it, but whoever loses his life for My sake will find it. For what profit is it to a man if he gains the whole world, and loses his own soul? Or what will a man give in exchange for his soul? For the Son of Man will come in the glory of His Father with His angels, and then He will reward each according to his works."

LOST AND FOUND

In this passage, Jesus shares with His disciples the three laws of discipleship:

1. *Law of self-denial*: "let him deny himself"
2. *Law of sacrifice*: "take up his cross"
3. *Law of submission*: "follow Me"

But the Lord does not just leave them with these responsibilities. He qualifies them by pointing out the rewards that belong to those who are disciples:

1. *Permanence of discipleship:* "For whoever desires to save his life will lose it," meaning that joy and fulfillment are found when we exchange our lives for the life of Christ.

2. *Price of discipleship:* "What profit is it . . . if he gains the whole world, and loses his own soul?" We all get only one chance to live by faith as believers. It is priceless.

3. *Prize of discipleship:* "He will reward each according to his works."

QUESTIONS

What It Says: In this passage, what is lost, and what is found?

_____

_____

_____

What It Means: Are the rewards worth the cost? List the pros and cons.

_____

_____

_____

What It Means for You: Have you ever given thought to the worth of your soul? What about the souls of others?

_____

_____

_____

36

LUKE 11:1–4

Now it came to pass, as He was praying in a certain place, when He ceased, that one of His disciples said to Him, "Lord, teach us to pray, as John also taught his disciples." So He said to them, "When you pray, say: Our Father in heaven, Hallowed be Your name. Your kingdom come. Your will be done On earth as it is in heaven. Give us day by day our daily bread. And forgive us our sins, For we also forgive everyone who is indebted to us. And do not lead us into temptation, But deliver us from the evil one."

GOD'S DELIVERANCE

In the Lord's Prayer, Jesus instructs us to pray that God will "deliver us from the evil one." But what are we really requesting? The Psalms provide some categories that can help us understand the kinds of deliverance that we can expect of God:

- *Deliverance from persecution.* "Deliver me, lest they tear me like a lion, rending me in pieces" (Ps. 7:1–2).
- *Deliverance from peril.* "Deliver me from the sword . . . Save me from the lion's mouth" (Ps. 22:19–21).
- *Deliverance from personal adversaries.* "Deliver me from the hands of my enemies" (Ps. 31:15).
- *Deliverance from the power of fear.* "I sought the Lord, and He heard me. And delivered me from all my fears" (Ps. 34:4).

- *Deliverance from the power of evil.* "Deliver me from all my transgressions; Do not make me the reproach of the foolish" (Ps. 39:8).

QUESTIONS

What It Says: What did Jesus invite His disciples to pray about?

_____

_____

_____

What It Means: Which items are about us? Which are about God?

_____

_____

_____

_____

What It Means for You: Do you share any of David's fears? How would you personalize your prayer for deliverance?

_____

_____

_____

_____

37

MATTHEW 25:35–40

"I was hungry and you gave Me food; I was thirsty and you gave Me drink; I was a stranger and you took Me in; I was naked and you clothed Me; I was sick and you visited Me; I was in prison and you came to Me." Then the righteous will answer Him, saying, "Lord, when did we see You hungry and feed You, or thirsty and give You drink? When did we see You a stranger and take You in, or naked and clothe You? Or when did we see You sick, or in prison, and come to You?" And the King will answer and say to them, "Assuredly, I say to you, inasmuch as you did it to one of the least of these My brethren, you did it to Me."

THE LEAST OF THESE

How do we express our love to the One who loved us with the gift of His own life? First, we love Jesus by obeying His commandments. Jesus says, "He who has My commandments and keeps them, it is he who loves Me" (John 14:21). We also love Jesus by serving others. "By this all will know that you are My disciples, if you have love for one another" (John 13:35). Finally, we love Jesus by showing compassion to the needy. We read in Matthew 25, "Assuredly, I say to you, inasmuch as you did it to one of the least of these My brethren, you did it to Me" (v. 4).

The Bible promises that as we love Jesus in these ways, He will make Himself known to us, and He will make His home with us. We will honor Christ's name in the world as we love Him by loving and serving others.

QUESTIONS

What It Says: What kinds of people are in need in this passage?

_____

_____

_____

_____

What It Means: How does the King confuse those who will enter His kingdom? Why are they surprised?

_____

_____

_____

_____

What It Means for You: Do your own responsibilities keep you from noticing the needs of those around you? How has this story changed your outlook?

_____

_____

_____

_____

_____

38

MATTHEW 20:25–28

But Jesus called them to Himself and said, "You know that the rulers of the Gentiles lord it over them, and those who are great exercise authority over them. Yet it shall not be so among you; but whoever desires to become great among you, let him be your servant. And whoever desires to be first among you, let him be your slave—just as the Son of Man did not come to be served, but to serve, and to give His life a ransom for many."

THE UPSIDE-DOWN KINGDOM

The world's approach to leadership and the church's approach to leadership are two different things. In the world, a person starts a job on the lower level and keeps working up. Then, after arriving at the top, the person looks down at everyone who is serving and says, "I'm the boss, and all these people do my bidding." But Jesus declares that anyone who desires to be a leader in the kingdom of God must take this model and turn it upside down. The question in the kingdom of God is not how many people are serving the leaders, but how many people are the leaders serving? In the kingdom of God, the way up is the way down. The more useful people want to be to Him, the greater responsibility they have to serve others.

QUESTIONS

What It Says: Why did Jesus say He came?

_____

_____

_____

_____

What It Means: What does greatness look like in the kingdom God has established?

_____

_____

_____

_____

_____

What It Means for You: Where do you serve? Within your congregation, who is serving you?

_____

_____

_____

_____

_____

39

JOHN 12:1–3

Then, six days before the Passover, Jesus came to Bethany, where Lazarus was who had been dead, whom He had raised from the dead. There they made Him a supper; and Martha served, but Lazarus was one of those who sat at the table with Him. Then Mary took a pound of very costly oil of spikenard, anointed the feet of Jesus, and wiped His feet with her hair. And the house was filled with the fragrance of the oil.

DEVOTED FRIEND

The Hebrew expression of sitting at one's feet meant to learn from that person. The idiom describes a person submitting to another one's teaching, authority, and ways of life. Mary was humble and teachable (Luke 10:39). According to John, she showed her love for Jesus at His feet three other times (John 11:2, 32; 12:3). From Mary we learn that it is more important to be occupied *with* Christ than to be occupied *for* Him.

Mary was also generous. He own brother had died, yet she had not used her costly perfume for his burial. Instead, Jesus explained that she had saved it "for the day of My burial." This devoted friend lavished her most precious possession on her Savior. She took the most honored part of her body (her hair) and used it to clean the lowliest and dirtiest part of Jesus' body (His feet). In this way, she showed Him her complete submission and love.

QUESTIONS

What It Says: This stay-over becomes something more than dinner with friends. What does Mary do that changes the whole atmosphere?

_____

_____

_____

_____

What It Means: Who benefited from this sacrifice?

_____

_____

_____

_____

What It Means for You: What are your most precious possessions? How can you give them to God?

_____

_____

_____

_____

_____

_____

40

MATTHEW 21:7–9

They brought the donkey and the colt, laid their clothes on them, and set Him on them. And a very great multitude spread their clothes on the road; others cut down branches from the trees and spread them on the road. Then the multitudes who went before and those who followed cried out, saying: "Hosanna to the Son of David! 'Blessed is He who comes in the name of the Lord!' Hosanna in the highest!"

PALM LEAVES

"When the chief priests and scribes saw the wonderful things that He did, and the children crying out in the temple and saying, 'Hosanna to the Son of David!' they were indignant" (Matt. 21:15). Since the days of the Maccabean revolt (some two hundred years before Jesus' Triumphal Entry), palm leaves had represented independence to the Jewish people. Whenever they felt the oppression of Rome, the Jewish people waved palms ("branches from the trees") as a way of saying, "We shall be free someday." Jewish coins from that period all bear the image of a palm branch. So when the people waved palms at Christ's Triumphal Entry into Jerusalem, they expressed their hope that the Messiah was in the city, taking control, throwing off Roman bondage, and setting them free to be the mighty nation they once were (Zech. 9:9). He did set them free—just not in the way they expected.

QUESTIONS

What It Says: How did the people gathering in Jerusalem greet Jesus?

_____

_____

_____

_____

What It Means: Jesus was fulfilling Zechariah's prophecy. Was he also fulfilling these peoples' expectations?

_____

_____

_____

_____

What It Means for You: The things we want may be the very things God wants for us. Journal about a time when a prayer was answered or a need was fulfilled in a way you didn't expect.

_____

_____

_____

_____

_____

41

JOHN 13:3–5

Jesus, knowing that the Father had given all things into His hands, and that He had come from God and was going to God, rose from supper and laid aside His garments, took a towel and girded Himself. After that, He poured water into a basin and began to wash the disciples' feet, and to wipe them with the towel with which He was girded.

HUMBLE SERVICE

In Jewish culture, washing another person's feet was not the work of the typical house servant but was reserved for the lowest type of slave. As guests arrived at the home, the slave would kneel near a basin of water, remove the guests' sandals, and wash their feet. Then the slave would dry the guests' feet and replace the sandals.

Peter tried to spare Jesus. "Then He came to Simon Peter. And Peter said to Him, 'Lord, are You washing my feet?' Jesus answered and said to him, 'What I am doing you do not understand now, but you will know after this'" (John 13:6–7). More than anything else, this is what living as a Christian means: serving, giving, feeding others, which means serving Jesus (Matt. 25:40). Many Christians still practice foot washing today as a symbolic act of humble service.

QUESTIONS

What It Says: What role did Jesus take?

_____

_____

_____

_____

What It Means: Why would Peter and the other disciples have protested against this turn of events?

_____

_____

_____

_____

What It Means for You: The example has been set. How can you follow it in your own life? Be specific.

_____

_____

_____

_____

_____

42

MARK 14:32–36

Then they came to a place which was named Gethsemane; and He said to His disciples, "Sit here while I pray." And He took Peter, James, and John with Him, and He began to be troubled and deeply distressed. Then He said to them, "My soul is exceedingly sorrowful, even to death. Stay here and watch." He went a little farther, and fell on the ground, and prayed that if it were possible, the hour might pass from Him. And He said, "Abba, Father, all things are possible for You. Take this cup away from Me; nevertheless, not what I will, but what You will."

ANGUISH

In the Garden of Gethsemane, Jesus felt a depth of emotion that is hard to describe. Mark uses several terms to picture His anguished frame of mind: "troubled," "deeply distressed," and "exceedingly sorrowful." Together these words paint a picture of someone in an acute state of emotional distress. Even Jesus described Himself as "overwhelmed with sorrow, even to the point of death." He did not approach Calvary in a coolly detached or unemotional state of mind but instead anticipated these events with intense emotions.

Some people may wonder: Jesus had already staunchly predicted His death; why does He now have such emotion at the prospect of death? Was it fear? No. His emotion was because He was about to undergo something even bigger than mere physical death: He was preparing to take on the sins of the world.

QUESTIONS

What It Says: At a time like this, did Jesus want to be totally alone?

_____

_____

_____

_____

What It Means: Who did He want with Him? Who did He speak with?

_____

_____

_____

_____

What It Means for You: Where do you turn during troubling times? Be honest. Who can you rely on in the face of a crisis?

_____

_____

_____

_____

_____

_____

43

JOHN 18:37

Pilate therefore said to Him, "Are You a king then?" Jesus answered, "You say rightly that I am a king. For this cause I was born, and for this cause I have come into the world, that I should bear witness to the truth. Everyone who is of the truth hears My voice."

"ARE YOU A KING?"

Pilate knew he wasn't dealing with a criminal. Jesus wasn't a threat to Rome, but he was a King. And what a King!

- *He Is the King of the Jews*. "Where is He who has been born King of the Jews?" (Matt. 2:2)
- *He Is the King of Righteousness*. Jesus was prefigured by Melchizedek, translated "King of Righteousness" (Heb. 7:1–2).
- *He Is the King of Peace*. Jesus is compared with the king of Salem, which means "King of Peace" (Heb 7:2).
- *He Is the King Over All the Earth*. "And the LORD shall be King over all the earth" (Zech. 14:4, 8–9).
- *He is the King of Glory.* King David cries, "Who is this King of glory? The Lord strong and mighty" (Ps. 24:8).
- *He is King of Kings and Lord of Lords.* The book of Revelation twice gives this ultimate designation to our Lord (Rev. 17:14, 19:16). He is king not just of the Jews, but of the entire universe.

QUESTIONS

What It Says: Pilate's question is blunt. What is Jesus' equally straightforward answer?

_____

_____

_____

_____

What It Means: How far-reaching is Jesus' authority?

_____

_____

_____

_____

What It Means for You: Jesus' followers are a part of this kingdom. What can we tell about our homeland based on the titles of our King?

_____

_____

_____

_____

_____

44

MARK 15:12–15

Pilate answered and said to them again, "What then do you want me to do with Him whom you call the King of the Jews?" So they cried out again, "Crucify Him!" Then Pilate said to them, "Why, what evil has He done?" But they cried out all the more, "Crucify Him!" So Pilate, wanting to gratify the crowd, released Barabbas to them; and he delivered Jesus, after he had scourged Him, to be crucified.

WHO CRUCIFIED JESUS?

The Romans killed Jesus. Pilate, the Roman governor, could have freed Jesus, but to preserve his standing with the mob, he delivered Jesus to be crucified (Mark 15:15; John 18–19).

The Jews killed Jesus. They cried, "His blood *be* on us and on our children" (Matt. 27:25). And Peter later pointed his finger at them in Acts 2:23 and said, "You have taken by lawless hands, have crucified, and put to death."

God killed Jesus. "Yet we esteemed Him stricken, Smitten by God, and afflicted" (Isa. 53:4). "Yet it pleased the LORD to bruise Him; He has put *Him* to grief" (Isa. 53:10). "Him, being delivered by the determined purpose and foreknowledge of God" (Acts 2:23). God did it!

I killed Jesus. Who crucified Jesus? We did it. All of us (Isa. 53:5). Every single one of us. My sins nailed Him to the cross. He died for me.

QUESTIONS

What It Says: Did Jesus descrve His sentence?

_____

_____

_____

_____

What It Means: Who was to blame for the Crucifixion?

_____

_____

_____

_____

What It Means for You: You are part of the reason Jesus had to die. How does knowing this affect how you think about something that happened so long ago?

_____

_____

_____

_____

_____

_____

45

MATTHEW 27:46–50

And about the ninth hour Jesus cried out with a loud voice, saying, "Eli, Eli, lama sabachthani?" that is, "My God, My God, why have You forsaken Me?" Some of those who stood there, when they heard that, said, "This Man is calling for Elijah!" Immediately one of them ran and took a sponge, filled it with sour wine and put it on a reed, and offered it to Him to drink. The rest said, "Let Him alone; let us see if Elijah will come to save Him." And Jesus cried out again with a loud voice, and yielded up His spirit.

CALL FOR ELIJAH

As Jesus cried out the tortured words, Eli, Eli, lama sabachthani, some who heard him misunderstood Him (Ps. 22:1). The Aramaic word eloi can easily be mistaken for the prophet Elijah's name. Some observers callously wondered if Elijah would come to help Him, not understanding that if the prophet made such an appearance, fire from heaven would likely accompany him to burn up the enemies of the Lord, just as it had his own adversaries centuries before (2 Kings 1:10, 12).

Jesus remained in control of His destiny: in absolute conformity to His Father's will, He chose the moment of His baptism, His triumphal entry, even His arrest and crucifixion. And finally He chose the moment when He yielded up His spirit (John 19:30), fulfilling His words: "I lay down My life that I may take it again. No one takes it from Me, but I lay it down of Myself" (John 10:17–18).

QUESTIONS

What It Says: What kinds of people gathered to watch Jesus die? Was this any different than when people gathered to watch Him teach?

_____

_____

_____

_____

What It Means: How did Jesus treat death? How should we?

_____

_____

_____

_____

What It Means for You: Why isn't showing up enough? How far will curiosity carry you?

_____

_____

_____

_____

_____

46

LUKE 23:44–46

Now it was about the sixth hour, and there was darkness over all the earth until the ninth hour. Then the sun was darkened, and the veil of the temple was torn in two. And when Jesus had cried out with a loud voice, He said, "Father, 'into Your hands I commit My spirit.'" Having said this, He breathed His last.

AFTERSHOCKS

Jerusalem reverberated with the aftershocks of Christ's crucifixion. Everyone knew about the execution, and everyone had an opinion about the late prophet from Galilee. His death relieved many; His teachings and miracle-workings had disrupted and traumatized their lives. Now, with His passing, they could get on with everyday living.

For others, however, the death of the Lord brought mourning and despair. They had believed that He was their Messiah, prophesied from the Old Testament. They had hoped and trusted that His coming would deliver them from the dominion of Rome. But the object of their hopes, the One they had believed in, had been lifted up on a cross and forced to hang there until dead by the very Roman Empire He was supposed to conquer. Their hope was gone; their Messiah was dead. And they hid in darkened rooms, devastated and shocked.

QUESTIONS

What It Says: What miraculous events occurred at the same time as Jesus' death?

_____

_____

_____

_____

What It Means: How does grief affect faith?

_____

_____

_____

_____

What It Means for You: Are you afraid of death? Journal the things you don't want to leave unfinished.

_____

_____

_____

_____

_____

_____

47

MATTHEW 27:57–60

Now when evening had come, there came a rich man from Arimathea, named Joseph, who himself had also become a disciple of Jesus. This man went to Pilate and asked for the body of Jesus. Then Pilate commanded the body to be given to him. When Joseph had taken the body, he wrapped it in a clean linen cloth, and laid it in his new tomb which he had hewn out of the rock; and he rolled a large stone against the door of the tomb, and departed.

JOSEPH OF ARIMATHEA

All four Gospels tell of Joseph of Arimathea, and each reveals something the others do not. He was a rich man (Matt. 27:57) and a prominent council member (Mark 15:43). He's described as a good and just man (Luke 23:50). Yet before Jesus' death, he was a secret disciple who had concealed his allegiance out of fear of his fellow Sanhedrin members (John 19:38).

After Christ's death, Joseph showed great courage when he risked his reputation and livelihood—perhaps even his life—to ask Pilate for Jesus' body. "So he came and took the body of Jesus. . . . Then they took the body of Jesus, and bound it in strips of linen with the spices, as the custom of the Jews is to bury" (John 19:38, 40). Joseph of Arimathea used his own tomb to bury Jesus, a loving act of sacrifice and devotion for a quiet follower of Jesus.

QUESTIONS

What It Says: Jesus had followers from many walks of life. How many can you think of?

_____

_____

_____

_____

What It Means: What part did Joseph of Arimathea play in this drama?

_____

_____

_____

_____

What It Means for You: Was Joseph of Arimathea outspoken about his faith? The truth came out when this man stepped forward. In what ways have you taken similar risks?

_____

_____

_____

_____

48

MATTHEW 28:1–4

Now after the Sabbath, as the first day of the week began to dawn, Mary Magdalene and the other Mary came to see the tomb. And behold, there was a great earthquake; for an angel of the Lord descended from heaven, and came and rolled back the stone from the door, and sat on it. His countenance was like lightning, and his clothing as white as snow. And the guards shook for fear of him, and became like dead men.

BEYOND THE CROSS

Every year thousands of people climb a mountain in the Italian Alps, passing the "stations of the cross" to stand at an outdoor crucifix. One time a tourist noticed a little trail that led beyond the cross. He fought through the rough thicket and, to his surprise, came upon another shrine, one devoted to the empty tomb. It was neglected; the brush had grown up around it. Almost everyone had gone as far as the cross, but there they stopped.

Many people have made it to the cross and have known its despair and the heartbreak. Far too few have moved beyond the cross to find the real message of Easter—the message of the empty tomb. "Do not be afraid, for I know that you seek Jesus who was crucified. He is not here; for He is risen, as He said. Come, see the place where the Lord lay" (Matt. 28:5–6).

QUESTIONS

What It Says: After a weekend of despair and heartbreak, what miracle did Sunday morning bring?

_____

_____

_____

_____

What It Means: Why does a gruesome death grab more attention than a good life?

_____

_____

_____

_____

What It Means for You: If there's no greater love than to die for a friend, what does it take to live for your Friend?

_____

_____

_____

_____

_____

49

MATTHEW 27:62–65

On the next day, which followed the Day of Preparation, the chief priests and Pharisees gathered together to Pilate, saying, "Sir, we remember, while He was still alive, how that deceiver said, 'After three days I will rise.' Therefore command that the tomb be made secure until the third day, lest His disciples come by night and steal Him away, and say to the people, 'He has risen from the dead.' So the last deception will be worse than the first." Pilate said to them, "You have a guard; go your way, make it as secure as you know how."

SET A GUARD

Jewish officials panicked because thousands were following Christ. They heard Jesus predict that He would rise on the third day, so they had to make sure He was put away for good. Although the idea that the disciples stole the body of Jesus might explain the missing corpse, the idea is more absurd than any other theory put forth to explain away the Resurrection.

A Roman guard unit consisted of four to sixteen men. Normally, four men were stationed immediately in front of the object they were to protect, while the other twelve slept in a semicircle in front of these four. Every four hours, a new unit of four was awakened, and those who had been keeping watch went to sleep. This routine went on around the clock. To steal what these guards were protecting, thieves would first have to walk over those who were asleep and then deal with the guards who were not.

QUESTIONS

What It Says: Who assigned Roman guards to the tomb?

_____

_____

_____

_____

_____

What It Means: Why were these guards necessary?

_____

_____

_____

_____

What It Means for You: Can anyone prevent God from acting? Have you ever been in a place where you needed a miracle?

_____

_____

_____

_____

_____

50

MARK 15:46

Then he bought fine linen, took Him down, and wrapped Him in the linen. And he laid Him in a tomb which had been hewn out of the rock, and rolled a stone against the door of the tomb.

THE SEAL

Matthew records that the soldiers "went and made the tomb secure, sealing the stone" (Matt. 27:66). The seal could be placed on the stone only in the presence of the Roman guards who were in charge. The procedure was designed to prevent anyone from tampering with the contents of the grave. After the guards inspected the tomb and rolled the stone in place, a cord was stretched across the rock. This was fastened at either end with sealing clay. Then the clay packs were stamped with the official signet of the Roman governor.

Despite these precautions, on Resurrection morning the seal was broken because the stone had been removed from the opening of the tomb. "And behold, there was a great earthquake; for an angel of the Lord descended from heaven, and came and rolled back the stone from the door, and sat on it" (Matt. 28:2).

QUESTIONS

What It Says: How many different people verified that Jesus was in that garden tomb?

_____

_____

_____

_____

What It Means: In an effort to prevent fraud, what did the officials actually provide?

_____

_____

_____

_____

What It Means for You: Describe a time when you faced an "impossible" obstacle? What did you learn about yourself and about God?

_____

_____

_____

_____

51

JOHN 20:1–6

Now on the first day of the week Mary Magdalene went to the tomb early, while it was still dark, and saw that the stone had been taken away from the tomb. Then she ran and came to Simon Peter, and to the other disciple, whom Jesus loved, and said to them, "They have taken away the Lord out of the tomb, and we do not know where they have laid Him." Peter therefore went out, and the other disciple, and were going to the tomb. So they both ran together, and the other disciple outran Peter and came to the tomb first. And he, stooping down and looking in, saw the linen cloths lying there; yet he did not go in. Then Simon Peter came, following him, and went into the tomb.

HEAVY STONE

In Mark's account of the Resurrection, we are told that the stone placed in front of Jesus' tomb was extremely large (Mark 16:4). A groove was cut into the rock in front of early sepulchers to hold the stone that sealed them. This groove was cut so that its lowest part lay right in front of the tomb's opening. When the wedge holding the stone was removed, the stone would roll down the groove and wedge itself into place, closing the opening into the grave.

On that Sunday morning, not only was the stone no longer in front of the tomb, it had been moved out of the groove and was some distance from where it would have been had it been moved in the conventional way. In his Gospel, John uses a word that means, "to pick something up and carry it away" (John 20:1).

QUESTIONS

What It Says: How did the disciples react to Mary's news?

_____

_____

_____

_____

What It Means: At first, how did they try to explain away what they were seeing?

_____

_____

_____

_____

What It Means for You: Why do things need to make sense to you before you truly believe?

_____

_____

_____

_____

_____

52

MARK 16:1–6

Now when the Sabbath was past, Mary Magdalene, Mary the mother of James, and Salome bought spices, that they might come and anoint Him. Very early in the morning, on the first day of the week, they came to the tomb when the sun had risen. And they said among themselves, "Who will roll away the stone from the door of the tomb for us?" But when they looked up, they saw that the stone had been rolled away—for it was very large. And entering the tomb, they saw a young man clothed in a long white robe sitting on the right side; and they were alarmed. But he said to them, "Do not be alarmed. You seek Jesus of Nazareth, who was crucified. He is risen! He is not here. See the place where they laid Him."

SEE THE PLACE

Everyone agrees that Jesus' tomb was empty—even those who deny the Gospel accounts. The accounts of the Resurrection would never have been believed if people had found the body still there. So the question has always been: What became of it? Would the authorities deliberately remove the body to prevent the disciples from claiming that He had risen? This is difficult to believe. In that case, the authorities would have immediately produced the body to shut down the new movement and silence the apostles' proclamations.

Did the disciples steal the body as part of a hoax, an attempt to deceive people into believing that He had risen? This theory is impossible, for the disciples were prepared to suffer and die for the gospel, and people do not become martyrs for something they know is a lie.

QUESTIONS

What It Says: Why were the women going to the tomb?

_____

_____

_____

_____

What It Means: What news were these startled ladies the first to hear?

_____

_____

_____

_____

What It Means for You: Good news travels fast. Often, bad news travels faster. Is the Good News of the Gospel nothing more than old news? On a scale of 1 to 10 (10 being best), how often is your conversation filled with gossip and complaints? Using the same scale, rate how often you speak to others about the things of the Lord. What can you do to make changes?

_____

_____

_____

53

JOHN 20:3–8

Peter therefore went out, and the other disciple, and were going to the tomb. So they both ran together, and the other disciple outran Peter and came to the tomb first. And he, stooping down and looking in, saw the linen cloths lying there; yet he did not go in. Then Simon Peter came, following him, and went into the tomb; and he saw the linen cloths lying there, and the handkerchief that had been around His head, not lying with the linen cloths, but folded together in a place by itself. Then the other disciple, who came to the tomb first, went in also; and he saw and believed.

THE SHROUD

In the most literal sense, the grave was not empty because the grave clothes were still there. When John leaned over and looked into the tomb, he saw something so startling that he did not enter: where the body of Jesus had lain were His grave clothes, in the form of a body but slightly caved in and empty. John never got over this sight. The first thing that stuck in the minds of the disciples was not the empty tomb but the empty grave clothes—undisturbed in their form and position.

This sign of Easter eliminates the theory that the body was stolen—no thief would have left the linen grave clothes there. It also eliminates the theory that Jesus resuscitated Himself and walked out of the grave. How could He leave the grave clothes in the shape of His body in the tomb? One glance at Jesus' burial clothes proved the reality of the Resurrection.

QUESTIONS

What It Says: Which two disciples raced to the tomb?

_____

_____

_____

_____

What It Means: Why was the presence of the grave clothes so baffling?

_____

_____

_____

_____

_____

What It Means for You: This was enough to convince John. Do you remember what first convinced you to believe?

_____

_____

_____

_____

_____

54

JOHN 20:24–28

Now Thomas, called the Twin, one of the twelve, was not with them when Jesus came. The other disciples therefore said to him, "We have seen the Lord." So he said to them, "Unless I see in His hands the print of the nails, and put my finger into the print of the nails, and put my hand into His side, I will not believe." And after eight days His disciples were again inside, and Thomas with them. Jesus came, the doors being shut, and stood in the midst, and said, "Peace to you!" Then He said to Thomas, "Reach your finger here, and look at My hands; and reach your hand here, and put it into My side. Do not be unbelieving, but believing." And Thomas answered and said to Him, "My Lord and my God!"

MY HANDS, MY SIDE

Jesus appeared to the disciples when they were gathered behind closed doors. "Then, the same day at evening, being the first day of the week, when the doors were shut where the disciples were assembled, for fear of the Jews, Jesus came and stood in the midst, and said to them, 'Peace be with you.' When He had said this, He showed them His hands and His side. Then the disciples were glad when they saw the Lord" (John 20:19–20).

When Thomas, who had been absent, heard about Jesus' appearance, he said that he would not believe unless he could see Jesus and His scars for himself. Jesus graciously accommodated Thomas' desire and returned to the disciples the following Sunday. The scars so convinced His doubting disciple and the others that they believed and were transformed.

QUESTIONS

What It Says: What did Thomas miss?

_____

_____

_____

What It Means: We often use the phrase "too good to be true." Can you understand his reservations?

_____

_____

_____

What It Means for You: Jesus returned to see Thomas. What does that tell us about our Savior?

_____

_____

_____

_____

_____

55

JOHN 20:14–16

Now when she had said this, she turned around and saw Jesus standing there, and did not know that it was Jesus. Jesus said to her, "Woman, why are you weeping? Whom are you seeking?" She, supposing Him to be the gardener, said to Him, "Sir, if You have carried Him away, tell me where You have laid Him, and I will take Him away." Jesus said to her, "Mary!" She turned and said to Him, "Rabboni!" (which is to say, Teacher).

SIGHTINGS

In 1 Corinthians 15, Paul summarizes Jesus' appearances after His resurrection. "He was seen by Cephas, then by the twelve. After that He was seen by over five hundred brethren at once, of whom the greater part remain to the present, but some have fallen asleep. After that He was seen by James, then by all the apostles. Then last of all He was seen by me also, as by one born out of due time" (1 Cor. 15:5–8).

The New Testament records Jesus showing Himself alive to certain individuals, to the gathered disciples, and to more than five hundred brethren at once. Many of these people would still be alive when Paul wrote his words in AD 54. One writer has noted that if you brought all of these witnesses into a courtroom and gave each only six minutes to testify, you would still have over 50 hours of testimony to the reality of the risen Christ.

QUESTIONS

What It Says: What assumptions did Mary make about the man who addressed her in the garden?

_____

_____

_____

_____

_____

What It Means: When did she recognize Jesus?

_____

_____

_____

_____

_____

What It Means for You: Do you know the voice of your Shepherd?

_____

_____

_____

_____

_____

56

JOHN 20:27–29

Then He said to Thomas, "Reach your finger here, and look at My hands; and reach your hand here, and put it into My side. Do not be unbelieving, but believing." And Thomas answered and said to Him, "My Lord and my God!" Jesus said to him, "Thomas, because you have seen Me, you have believed. Blessed are those who have not seen and yet have believed."

QUESTIONS AND DOUBTS

We can learn much from "Doubting Thomas." First, Jesus didn't rebuke him for his questions. He simply answered them. We should never shy away from asking questions. Second, Thomas went on to serve God. The church is there today because of this man who asked a question. Doubter? Not really. The questions were the beginning of his journey, and he went on to bear much fruit.

Thomas saw and believed, and Jesus affirmed his belief. But then He added, Blessed *are* those who have not seen and *yet* have believed. If the Gospel events happened today in your presence, would you believe? If so, why does the passage of time change anything? The historical veracity of the biblical accounts has been established, so you can have as much confidence believing without seeing as those who saw and believed.

QUESTIONS

What It Says: Who does Jesus say will be blessed?

_____

_____

_____

_____

_____

What It Means: What is the foundation of your faith?

_____

_____

_____

_____

_____

What It Means for You: What questions do you wish you could ask Jesus Himself?

_____

_____

_____

_____

_____

57

LUKE 8:1–3

Now it came to pass, afterward, that He went through every city and village, preaching and bringing the glad tidings of the kingdom of God. And the twelve were with Him, and certain women who had been healed of evil spirits and infirmities—Mary called Magdalene, out of whom had come seven demons, and Joanna the wife of Chuza, Herod's steward, and Susanna, and many others who provided for Him from their substance.

MARY MAGDALENE

Wherever a group of women is named, Mary Magdalene's name appears first on the list, probably indicating that she was the leader of the group, if not its most important member. Not to be confused with the woman who anointed Jesus' head in Luke 7:37 or the sister of Lazarus, Jesus cast seven demons out of this Mary (Luke 8:2). She came from a city on the Sea of Galilee called Magdala, so "Magdalene" became her surname.

The Bible presents her as a pure, though deeply afflicted, woman. After Jesus healed her, she became one of the Lord's most dedicated disciples, remaining with Him throughout his trial, crucifixion, and burial. When all Jesus' followers abandoned Him on the cross, Mary Magdalene stayed nearby (Luke 23:49). She was the first to see the empty tomb and the first to worship the risen Christ (Luke 24:1; Matt. 28:1; Mark 16:1–2).

QUESTIONS

What It Says: How did Jesus' friendship with Mary Magdalene begin?

_____

_____

_____

_____

What It Means: Her faith kept her close to her Savior, even during the worst. What must it have been like, watching Jesus die on a cross?

_____

_____

_____

_____

What It Means for You: How would you describe your own devotion to Jesus?

_____

_____

_____

_____

_____

58

LUKE 22:54, 59–62

Having arrested Him, they led Him and brought Him into the high priest's house. But Peter followed at a distance . . . Then after about an hour had passed, another confidently affirmed, saying, "Surely this fellow also was with Him, for he is a Galilean." But Peter said, "Man, I do not know what you are saying!" Immediately, while he was still speaking, the rooster crowed. And the Lord turned and looked at Peter. And Peter remembered the word of the Lord, how He had said to him, "Before the rooster crows, you will deny Me three times." So Peter went out and wept bitterly.

DO YOU LOVE ME?

Peter's life teaches us some important lessons for anyone who longs for the opportunity to make things right. From his mistakes, we can learn how to prepare for a second chance:

- *Recognition:* Accept what you have done.
- *Remorse:* Experience a time of great sorrow at the full impact of your disobedience.
- *Repentance:* Face up to what you have done, dealing with it according to God's standards and saying, "I will not do that again. I will walk the other way."
- *Reflection:* See the implications of your action and the possibility of a renewed future.
- *Reassignment:* Accept the opportunity to serve God again.

Jesus said to Peter, "'Simon, son of Jonah, do you love Me?' Peter was grieved because He said to him the third time, 'Do you love Me?' And he said to Him, 'Lord, You know all things; You know that I love You'" (John 21:17).

QUESTIONS

What It Says: In this case, why was it so terrible for Peter to live up to Jesus' expectations?

_____

_____

_____

What It Means: When have you ever tasted the bitterness of regret? Be specific.

_____

_____

_____

What It Means for You: How do Peter's mistakes make it easier to move past your own?

_____

_____

_____

_____

59

JOHN 20:30–31

And truly Jesus did many other signs in the presence of His disciples, which are not written in this book; but these are written that you may believe that Jesus is the Christ, the Son of God, and that believing you may have life in His name.

THE MIRACLES OF JESUS CHRIST

John used the word *sign* seventeen times in his Gospel to convey that these mighty works of Jesus were done for the purpose of teaching deep, underlying lessons to His disciples and to others who would hear of His miracles. It is a word that explains John's expressed purpose for writing the Gospel, as recorded in John 20:30–31. At the wedding at Cana, "This beginning of signs Jesus did in Cana of Galilee, and manifested His glory; and His disciples believed in Him" (John 2:11).

However, many chased after Him as a wonder-worker. "But although He had done so many signs before them, they did not believe in Him" (John 12:37). The miracles of John's Gospel are not important because they arouse wonder and amazement in our hearts. They are important because they point us to something beyond ourselves. They show us God at work.

QUESTIONS

What It Says: What was the entertainment value in following Jesus?

_____

_____

_____

_____

What It Means: John insists that these signs served a purpose. Why did so many miss it?

_____

_____

_____

_____

What It Means for You: The Gospels were written "that you might believe." Do you?

_____

_____

_____

_____

_____

60

MATTHEW 28:18–20

And Jesus came and spoke to them, saying, "All authority has been given to Me in heaven and on earth. Go therefore and make disciples of all the nations, baptizing them in the name of the Father and of the Son and of the Holy Spirit, teaching them to observe all things that I have commanded you; and lo, I am with you always, even to the end of the age." Amen.

MAKE DISCIPLES

Jesus refers to Himself as the Son of Man eighty times in the Gospels. This title derives from Daniel 7:13–14, where we read of "One like the Son of Man, coming with the clouds of heaven . . . His dominion is an everlasting dominion, which shall not pass away." Jesus calls to mind this portrayal of the Messiah, who takes on human form and then ascends to heaven and inherits the kingdom of God.

Before the Son of Man departs, He leaves the disciples with a commission that has not changed since the moment Jesus uttered it. Christians are to go, make disciples, baptizing them and teaching them to obey. And they are to accomplish all of this by His power and for His sake, through His Spirit. When followers of Christ are slow to share their faith or pour into the lives of others, it is often because they do not really take Jesus at His word: "I am with you always."

QUESTIONS

What It Says: What has been given to Jesus? How far does His dominion extend?

_____

_____

_____

_____

What It Means: Why do Jesus' last words hold a promise for you?

_____

_____

_____

_____

What It Means for You: How are you living out the Lord's last command to His followers?

_____

_____

_____

_____

_____

_____

WHAT IT SAYS. WHAT IT MEANS.
WHAT IT MEANS FOR YOU.

FEATURES OF
***THE JEREMIAH STUDY BIBLE*:**

- Unique book introductions
- 8,000+ study notes
- Hundreds of enriching word studies
- Historical insights
- Geographical and archaeological information
- Hundreds of sidebars plus a sidebar index for the entire Bible
- Nearly 100 charts and maps keyed to particular passages of Scripture
- Special Teacher's Topical Index listing the major topics, respective articles, and biblical references within *The Jeremiah Study Bible*
- 60+ *Essentials of the Christian Faith* articles
- 80+ page general concordance
- Thorough cross-references
- Smartphone and web links to online digital resources

NEW AND LIFE-CHANGING . . .

WHAT IT SAYS.
WHAT IT MEANS.
WHAT IT MEANS FOR YOU.

THE
JEREMIAH
STUDY BIBLE

NKJV
NEW KING JAMES VERSION®

DR. DAVID JEREMIAH

AVAILABLE NOW